REJECTION:

YOUR PATH TO GROWTH

AND SUCCESS

DR. KATIE T. MCDONOUGH

TABLE OF CONTENTS

INTRODUCTION

In the vibrant city of Serendal, Maya, a young woman with lofty artistic dreams, faced a formidable challenge. Rejection seemed to cast a long shadow over her aspirations, testing her determination and causing doubt to seep into her heart. She questioned whether her dreams were worth pursuing in the face of constant setbacks.

One fateful day, while wandering through a cozy bookstore nestled in the heart of Serendal, Maya stumbled upon a book titled "Rejection: Your Path to Growth and Success." Intrigued by the possibility of a different perspective, she eagerly took hold of the book and immersed herself in its pages.

As Maya delved deeper into its contents, she discovered a wealth of insightful stories and practical wisdom. The book revealed the transformative power of embracing rejection and how it could pave the way to personal growth and success. Inspired and motivated, Maya realized that her journey had just begun, and she was determined to turn rejection into a catalyst for her dreams in the remarkable city of Serendal.

ACCEPTING REJECTION

Accepting a rejection means coming to terms with the fact that a specific goal or desired outcome has not been achieved. It means understanding and acknowledging the reality of the situation and recognizing that the desired result has not been met.

Accepting rejection is an important part of dealing with rejection. It is the most important phase in continuing on and finding other ways to achieve the desired outcome. It is likewise vital to perceive that a rejection does not necessarily mean that the goal is unattainable; it just means that a different approach or path might be more successful.

Accepting rejection also means being kind to oneself. It means recognizing that although the outcome was not what was hoped for, it does not mean that the situation is a failure. It is vital to permit oneself to feel the mistake and trouble related with the dismissal yet not to harp on it and to zero in rather on what can be gained from the experience and how to push ahead.

Finally, accepting a rejection means being able to accept the outcome and move on. It means understanding that although the desired outcome was not achieved, there are still other ways to progress and that it is feasible to accomplish the goal when another approach is taken. It is vital to perceive that albeit the initial outcome may have differed from what was expected, it does not mean the goal is out of reach.

A. Acknowledge Your Feelings

Recognizing your sentiments despite dismissal is a significant stage during the time spent tolerating it. This permits you to perceive and approve your feelings without permitting them to dominate and adversely influence your viewpoint.

When you acknowledge your feelings, being honest with yourself about them is important. Recognize how you feel about the rejection and why, rather than pushing those feelings away.

This might include requiring some investment to consider the This may involve taking some time to reflect on the rejection and its implications without judging yourself or your emotions.

Being thoughtful to yourself during this process is additionally significant. Dismissal can be a troublesome encounter, so rehearsing self-sympathy and understanding is significant. Recollect that you are in good company to feel as such and reserve the privilege to feel anyway you really want to adapt.

Finally, it is important to accept the rejection and move forward. Once you have acknowledged your feelings, it is important to recognize that rejection is part of life and to take steps to cope with it and move forward. This may involve setting goals or taking actionable steps to achieve your desired outcome.

By acknowledging your feelings in the face of rejection, you can process your experience healthily and move forward positively.

B. Allow Yourself to Grieve

When an individual has experienced rejection, they must allow themselves to grieve. Distress is a characteristic piece of the recuperating system and can help individuals understand their loss.

It is critical to remember that lamenting is certainly not an indication of shortcoming but rather of strength. Permitting oneself to handle the sentiments related to dismissal is a sound and vital piece of the mending system. It is essential to remember that feeling miserable, disappointed, irate, or hurt is OK. It is likewise critical to remember that these sentiments are not long-lasting and that traveling through them makes it feasible to come out the other side.

It is critical to respect your sentiments and steadily process them. This could mean conversing with a companion or relative, journaling about your viewpoints and sentiments, or finding an opportunity to accomplish something that gives you pleasure. It is critical to remember that everybody laments diversely and that there is no "correct" method for getting it done.

It is additionally vital to recall that the experience of dismissal doesn't characterize you or your value.It is ordinary for an individual to feel beat down after a dismissal, yet it is essential to remember that this is a mishap, as opposed to a super durable disappointment.Rejections can be a learning opportunity, and focusing on the positive aspects of the experience can be helpful.

At long last, it is vital to recall that it is okay to demand help and sponsorship while overseeing excusal. It is crucial to encircle yourself with individuals who can give you the assistance and understanding you truly need to mourn unequivocally.

C. Reflect on the Situation

Reflecting on the situation after accepting a rejection can be a difficult and emotional experience. It is important to recognize the emotions associated with rejection and not let them overwhelm you.

Finding the opportunity to think about the circumstances can assist you with acquiring knowledge about what might have been done another way and rolling out sure improvements later on.

The most important phase in pondering the circumstances is to make a stride back and think about what occurred. Consider your decisions and the moves you made before the dismissal. Consider the event that whatever you might have done in any other way might have had a positive result. This cycle can be troublesome and profound; however, it is essential to recall that dismissal doesn't reflect you or your value.

Another important step in reflecting on the situation is identifying any patterns or behaviors that may have contributed to the rejection. Consider any changes you could make in the future to increase your chances of success. This could involve working on communication skills, setting more achievable goals, or taking more risks.

Finally, taking the rejection in stride and involving it as a potential chance to learn and develop is important.

Rejections can be difficult to handle but can also be seen as a learning experience. Rejection can inform future decisions and can be a sign to focus on other opportunities. Accepting a rejection can be an emotionally trying experience, but taking the time to reflect on the situation can help to give insight and to make positive changes in the future.

D. Learn from the experience

Learning from the experience of accepting rejection is a valuable lesson that can help an individual become more resilient, confident, and booming. Rejection is a part of life and can be hard to accept, but it's important to remember that it is not a measure of personal worth or failure.

Instead, rejection should be seen as an opportunity to learn and grow. Accepting a rejection can help an individual recognize their assets and shortcomings and spotlight on regions for improvement. It can also provide insight into better navigating future challenges and obstacles.

By accepting a rejection, an individual can learn to focus on the positive and utilize the experience to develop self-awareness and resilience. It can help individuals become more confident in themselves and their abilities as they learn to trust their decision-making.

Accepting a rejection can also teach an individual the importance of taking risks and that failure can lead to success. It can help an individual understand that rejection doesn't spell almost certain doom for the excursion however can be a wellspring of inspiration and a chance to gain from errors and pursue better choices later on.

Overall, learning from the experience of accepting rejection is a valuable life lesson that can help an individual become more resilient, confident, and successful. It can help an individual recognize their strengths and weaknesses, focus on the positive, and take risks in the future. It can also provide insight into better navigating future challenges and obstacles.

II. Moving On from a Rejection

Moving on from a rejection can be difficult, especially if the rejection was unexpected. It is critical to recall that dismissals are a piece of life and can occur for some reasons. It is fundamental to have an inspiring viewpoint and to zero in on the future as opposed to choosing not to move on.

The first step in moving on from rejection is to accept it and recognize that it is a part of life. It is important to remember that rejection can happen for various reasons, and it is not necessarily a reflection of one's ability or self-worth. It implies a lot to make a step back and objectively analyze the situation to understand better why the rejection occurred.

The subsequent step is to find opportunity to process the rejection. It is important to acknowledge any feelings associated with the rejection, such as disappointment or sadness. Acknowledging these feelings and giving yourself time to grieve the rejection before moving on is important.

The third step is to track down ways of adapting to the dismissal. This might incorporate conversing with a confided in companion or relative, engaging in activities that bring joy or comfort, or seeking professional help. It is important to remember that there is no "correct" way to cope with a rejection, and finding methods that work for the individual is important.

The fourth step is to zero in on what's in store. As opposed to harping on the dismissal, it is vital to zero in on the subsequent stages and foster an arrangement for pushing ahead. This might include laying out new objectives or searching out new open doors. It is vital to recall that dismissals are a part of life and that, in every case, new doors open ahead.

At long last, practicing taking care of oneself is significant. It is vital to be delicate with oneself during this time and perceive that continuing on from dismissal will take time. It is vital to remember that dismissal doesn't characterize what one's identity is and that there are always new open doors ahead.

Moving on from rejection can be difficult, anyway, reviewing that is basic dismissal is important for life. It is important to accept the rejection, take the time to process it, find ways to cope, focus on the future, and practice self-care. With these steps, it is possible to move on from the rejection and to focus on the future.

A. Take Time for Yourself

Setting aside margin for yourself is a fundamental piece of continuing on from dismissal. It's vital to make an investment to consider the experience and survey how it affected you. It's likewise critical to make a few investments in taking care of oneself and to focus on exercises that make you cheerful and give you a feeling of fulfillment.

While setting aside margin for yourself, it's critical to be careful that you're currently recuperating and give yourself the space to do so. Do things that encourage you, like investing energy with companions, strolling, paying attention to music, perusing a book, or watching a film. Carving out margin for yourself after a dismissal is likewise a chance to check out your assets and once again center your energy around how you might push ahead.

It's critical to be delicate with yourself during this time, as handling the dismissal and the related emotions might be challenging. Be patient and good to yourself, as it could require a long investment to show up at a position of acknowledgment. It's additionally vital to remember that dismissal doesn't characterize you and that committing errors is okay.

Finally, reaching out to a trusted friend or family member can be helpful. A supportive network can encourage and help you move on from the rejection. It can also be beneficial to converse with an expert, like a specialist or guide, who can provide additional guidance and support.

Getting some margin to deal with yourself and process the rejection is essential to move on. Doing so can create a more positive outlook and encourage personal growth. Self-care, reflection, and support make it possible to come out of the situation more vigorous and resilient.

B. Stay positive and focus on what you can control.

When faced with rejection, staying positive and focusing on what you can control to move on is important. It is essential to recollect that dismissal doesn't characterize you, and it is important to recognize that this experience is a learning opportunity.

The first step in staying positive and moving on from rejection is to accept the experience and recognize that this experience is a part of life. Rejection can be difficult to process, and it is critical to advise yourself that it is typical to feel disheartened. Tolerating the experience can help you push ahead and center around the things you have some control over to continue on.

The following step is to zero in on the things that you have some command over. It is central to see that there are loads of things that you can deal with to help yourself in progressing forward from the excusal. You can focus in on developing new capacities, for instance, decisive reasoning and correspondence, that can help you with moving to a more elevated level from now into the foreseeable future. Besides, you can focus in on building areas of strength for a, strong organization of people who can help you in excess positive and spurred.

The third step is to celebrate your successes, whether big or small. Celebrating your accomplishments can assist you with remaining on track and spurred, and it can likewise help to remind you of your progress. Celebrating your successes can help to build your confidence and can help you to stay positive despite the rejection.

Finally, it is fundamental for focus in on the future and to see that excusal is a tiny bit of piece of your general cycle.. Remaining positive and zeroing in on what you have some control over can assist you with continuing on from the dismissal and keep pursuing accomplishing your objectives

Overall, staying positive and focusing on what you can control can help you move on from rejection and continue working towards achieving your goals. By accepting the experience, focusing on the things you can control, celebrating your successes, and focusing on the future, you can stay positive and motivated despite the rejection.

C. Take Action to Improve Your Situation

Take Action to Improve Your Situation is a concept that means that an individual should take proactive steps to address any rejection they may be facing. This means that the individual should move beyond the feelings of anger, hurt, and despair accompanying the disappointment of rejection and focus on the areas they can take action on to shape their lives positively.

The types of steps that individuals can take to improve their situation could include things such as:

1. Acknowledging and accepting the rejection: Accepting the reality of the situation is an important step in the process. This could involve taking some time out for self-reflection and understanding why you were rejected.

2. Developing a constructive mindset and attitude: This step involves utilizing positive self-talk and grounding yourself in the reality of the situation. Doing this could involve being proactive in seeking and making progress on advances in your career, studies, or hobbies that can help move your life in the desired direction.

3. Practicing self-care: This step involves engaging in activities that make you feel relaxed and supported. This could include spending time with supportive friends and family, attending support groups or therapy, or engaging in activities such as exercising.

4. Developing resilience and learning from the situation: This step involves looking back on the problem and becoming aware of any lessons you can understand that can help you better prepare for future experiences of rejection.

By taking steps to address the issue of rejection through these strategies, an individual has the opportunity to grow and develop more substantial and resilient responses to the disappointment associated with rejection. This can then prompt a more inspirational perspective for the future and encourage fearlessness.

D. Reach out for support

Reaching out for support when dealing with rejection is an important part of acceptance and healing. Accepting rejection can be a complicated process, so finding ways to cope is important. Connecting for help can be a difficult however compensating process. Certain individuals might wonder whether or not to look for help because of humiliation, disgrace, or culpability. It's memorable's vital that requesting help is an indication of solidarity and versatility, and it can assist with tracking down survival techniques and advance past dismissal.

When seeking support, having a clear idea of what type of help is needed can be helpful. Some individuals may be more comfortable talking to a close friend, family member, or therapist. Others may benefit from online support groups, hotlines, or counseling sessions. Any support system should provide a safe and non-judgmental atmosphere to communicate feelings and experiences openly.

Having somebody to converse with can be an incredible source of relief. People can share their feelings of hurt, anger, confusion, or any other emotions they may be feeling. This can help to normalize anxiety, create a sense of understanding, and build resilience.

When struggling with rejection, it's also important to remember that it's not a failure or a reflection of personal worth. Everybody encounters dismissal eventually, and it's critical to be caring to oneself and perceive the work as adapting. Taking deep breaths, practicing self-care, or engaging in activities that bring joy can also be beneficial.

Reaching out for support is important in accepting rejection and moving forward. With the right resources, people can find the strength to move past the pain of rejection.

E. Try not to take it personally.

Try not to take it personally is an expression often used to encourage someone to accept the potential of rejection without becoming emotionally affected by the outcome.

Accepting rejection can be difficult but it is an important part of life. When faced with a possible rejection, it is important to consider the situation objectively. Trying not to take it personally is a reminder not to allow rejection (or fear of rejection) to cause emotional distress or begin viewing oneself negatively.

It is helpful to consider why the rejection occurred. Was it on account of something you did or said? Was it beyond the other individual's control? Knowing the solution to this question can assist with understanding the circumstance better.

It is important to recognize that rejection is often not personal. Rejection may also occur due to factors that have nothing to do with the individual.

It can help to accept that rejection is part of life and not consider it a reflection of self-worth. Instead, focus on resilience in the face of rejection and learning from the experience.

When in the midst of rejection, self-care is important to restore equilibrium and support emotional recovery. This can involve activities such as:

- Socializing with friends and family.

- Taking up a hobby.

- Pursuing interests that bring joy.

At long last, recollecting that nobody is significant person is perfect, and rejection can be a chance to learn and grow. Recognize that everyone experiences rejection at some point in life and that with time comes understanding and acceptance.

III. Coping with Rejection

Coping with rejection can be a difficult and painful challenge.It is vital to comprehend that dismissal is an unavoidable piece of life and that it tends to be utilized as a chance for development.

Accepting and Learning From Rejection

Acknowledgment is the most vital phase in adapting to dismissal. It is vital to perceive that dismissal is a typical piece of life and that it's anything but an impression of what your identity is. By accepting the rejection and realizing that it is not a personal failure, it can be easier to move on and learn from the experience.

Self Care

It is vital to require investment to deal with yourself while adapting to dismissal.

This might incorporate investing energy with loved ones, participating in exercises that encourage you, or basically finding opportunity to investigate side interests or exercises that give you joy.

Communication

Sometimes it is beneficial to reach out to the person or situation that caused the rejection. This can help to provide clarity, resolve any misunderstandings, and come to an accommodation that works for both parties.

Creating Boundaries

Creating healthy boundaries is essential for coping with rejection. It means quite a bit to define clear limits in all everyday issues, like connections, work, and with acquaintances. Creating boundaries will allow you to be able to take control over situations and maintain your own sense of safety.

Self Reflection

Reflecting on the rejection experience can help to identify what may have gone wrong and how it can be avoided in the future. It is important to analyze the situation, your feelings and reactions, and what could have been done differently.

Rechanneling Negative Emotions

It can be helpful to rechannel any negative feelings into something positive. For example, if the rejection was due to a failed job application, it may help to center around the abilities and capabilities you have that led to the application being successful in any other situation.

Overall, it is important to remember that rejection is an inescapable piece of life and can provide valuable lessons and experiences. Coping with rejection can be a difficult challenge, but with determination and self-care, it is possible to move forward and become stronger.

A. Practice self-care

Practicing self-care in the context of accepting rejection is an important step to finding peace and moving on in life. Letting go of negative emotions can help you reclaim your sense of power and emotional well-being. Coming up next are several things that might end up being useful to you practice self-care in the context of accepting rejection:

1. Acceptance: It's important to accept the rejection and recognize that it is out of your control. Acceptance of the situation opens the door to shifting perspective toward the process of seeking better, healthier outcomes.

2. Feel your emotions: Allow yourself to feel the hurt, pain, and/or disappointment that comes with rejection. Acknowledge your emotions by labeling, expressing, and accepting them.

3. Talk to someone: Having a safe space to express emotions and to listen to supportive words helps. Conversing with a companion, relative, or specialist can help you gain clarity and move on with your life.

4. Reframe: Disassociate emotional pain from the situation and look for lessons, opportunities, and growth. Furthermore, reject the rejection and don't let it define you or your future.

5. Take Care of Yourself: Find simple ways to practice self-care like reading a book, taking a bath, or exercising. Small actions can help release the pain and make progress in accepting rejection.

6. Refocus your Energy: Redirect unproductive energy towards something productive. Doing something creative, focusing on self-improvement, or networking can help find better opportunities in life.

Practicing self-care in the context of accepting rejection is a gradual process. Being gentle and patient with yourself helps in allowing the emotions to be acknowledged and released. Remember that you are following some great people's example in your struggle and finding peace and happiness is the ultimate goal.

B. Focus on the things you enjoy.

Focusing on the things you enjoy is an important phrase to keep in mind when dealing with rejection. This phrase encourages an individual to keep looking forward and focus on the things that truly bring them joy.

Rejection is an inevitable part of life. Everybody manages it sooner or later, and while it can hurt, it is important to accept the rejection and recognize what it represents. Taking a moment to move on from the rejection and focusing on the things that make an individual happy can help cope with any feelings of negativity the rejection may bring. It is critical to recall that dismissal doesn't equal failure, so it is best to stay positive and continue to pursue the things that bring joy.

When it comes to redirecting focus after a rejection, it can help to make a list of the things that bring joy and happiness together. This list could include hobbies, sports, music, movies, books, journaling, spending time with family and friends, etc.

Focusing on and enjoying these activities can help an individual move on from the disappointment of a rejection.

It's also important to remember not to beat oneself up too much over a rejection. Dwelling on it will do nothing but bring down your mood and confidence. Everyone faces rejection, and everyone fails at some point. It's important to remember that this one rejection does not define who one is or what one can accomplish.

Focusing on the things you enjoy aims to help an individual focus on the positive and remember that rejections are part of life. It's important to accept the rejection, redirect focus, and move forward with the goal of achieving future success.

C. Limit Your Exposure to Rejection

Accepting rejection as part of life is incredibly difficult. No one likes hearing the word "no" or feeling insignificant. But often, the best way to manage your emotions in the face of rejection is to limit your exposure.

1. Shift your self-talk: One way to limit your exposure to rejection is by changing your self-talk. Rather than focusing on the negative, shift your thoughts towards what you could learn from the rejection. Identify any areas for improvement. This approach also helps to keep your focus away from negative, defeating thoughts and towards reflection and self-improvement.

2. Utilize support systems: Whether it's family, friends, or a therapist, connecting with supportive and understanding people can help soften the blow of rejection. It's also an opportunity to share experiences and gain new perspectives on the situation.

3. Set realistic expectations: Expecting too much from yourself and others can increase feelings of rejection. Recollecting that not all experiences is significant will turn out as desired. Setting realistic expectations can help to manage feelings of setbacks.

4. Take breaks: Rejection can quickly deplete one's energy and drive. Taking breaks throughout the day to engage in activities that are enjoyable and restorative can help to stay focused and motivated.

5. Stay present: Staying in the moment and slowing down can help to diminish feelings of rejection. Mindfulness activities such as progressive muscle relaxation and mindfulness meditations can help to become more grounded and connected to oneself.

Limiting your exposure to rejection is essential when it comes to maintaining emotional balance. The fact that none of us are makes it critical's vital immune to feeling disappointment and rejection, and that it's okay to feel how you are feeling. Through utilizing the tips provided, it's possible to navigate through difficult times and find the strength to keep going.

D. Find Alternative Ways to Achieve Your Goals

When you are faced with rejection, it can often feel like a blow to your self-esteem or self-worth. It is essential to recall that dismissal is simply a part of life and that it is a normal part of the way things are. Rejection can also be a great opportunity to look at your goals in a different way and find alternative ways of achieving them.

One of the most outstanding methodologies for managing rejection is to focus on the positive and find other options or paths that can help you accomplish the same goal. Taking the time to explore different paths can help you find a different way to reach your desired outcome. By breaking down your goal into its component steps, you can identify the different paths that need to be taken and then see if any of those paths have alternate routes that could get you to your goal.

Another option is to reassess your goals and see if they are still what you really want. Often times, when we experience rejection, it can be a sign that our goals may not actually be in line with our values and long-term objectives. Taking the time to re-evaluate and to make sure that our goals are still in line with what we truly desire is an important part of finding alternative ways to achieve our goals.

At long last, it is critical to make sure to be caring to yourself and to permit yourself to feel the feelings of the circumstance. Despite the fact that dismissal can be difficult to manage, it might be an extraordinary chance for self-awareness and self-reflection. Permitting yourself to truly get some margin to process and consider the experience can prompt tracking down elective ways of accomplishing your objectives. By taking a gander at the experience according to an alternate perspective, you might have the option to think of additional inventive and creative arrangements that could at last prompt achievement.

E. Find Humor in the Situation

To find humor in a circumstance, it is essential to perceive and acknowledge the dismissal. Dismissal can be troublesome and can be joined by a range of sentiments, like resentment, misery, and humiliation. It is essential to make an investment to be with and process your feelings. Whenever you have acknowledged the dismissal, it is feasible to begin to search for humor in the circumstances.

Humor can help to bring perspective, lighten the mood, and lead to creative solutions. Finding humor in a loss or rejection can also help to reduce feelings of resentment or regret.

Signs To Help You With Finding Humor In The Conditions:

• **Acknowledge your emotions:** Acknowledge your feelings and the reality of the situation. It is OK to experience disappointment and frustration.

• **Lighten up:** Look for the funny side of the situation by identifying the humor in what has happened.

• **Think positive:** Think of the situation as a learning experience and an opportunity for growth. Appreciate the opportunity for personal growth and development.

• **Break the tension**: Take a break and find ways to laugh. Poking fun at yourself or joking about the situation can help to reduce the tension.

• **See the big picture:** Focus on the long-term factors and recognize that, while one path may have closed, other paths may now open up.

By finding humor in the situation, you can shift your viewpoint and embrace optimism. This will empower you to push ahead and track down savvy fixes.

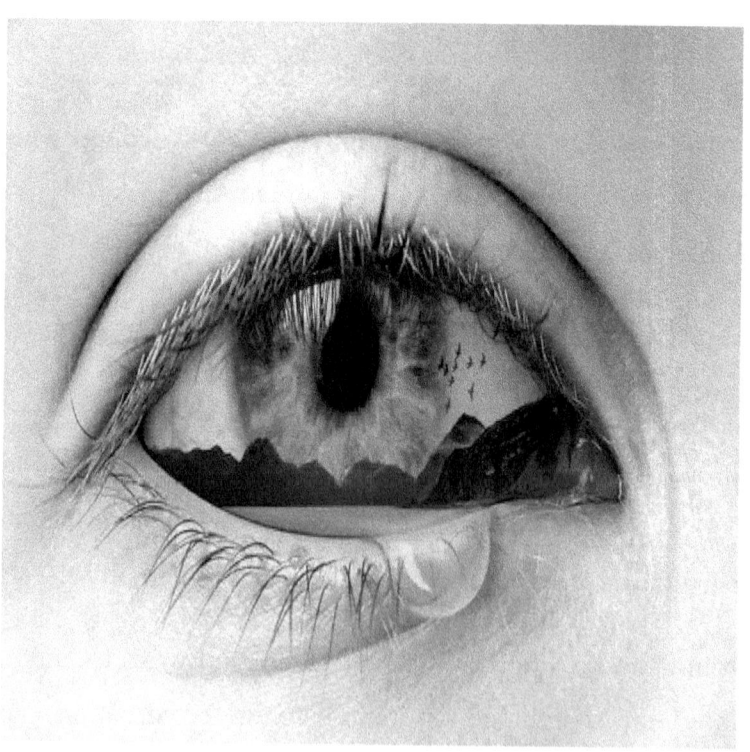

CONCLUSION

In the labyrinth of life, where rejection lurks at every turn, the "Rejection" book emerges as a guiding light, illuminating the transformative power of resilience and perseverance. Its pages bear the stories of countless souls who faced rejection head-on, only to emerge stronger and wiser.

Within these chapters lie the secrets to reframing rejection as a catalyst for growth, finding the courage to rise above setbacks, and embracing the lessons embedded in each "no." The "Rejection" book is a road-map to unlocking one's true potential by embracing rejection as a stepping stone to success.

As readers close the book, they are armed with an unwavering belief in their own worth, armed with the tools to navigate the treacherous seas of rejection with grace and determination. For in the face of rejection lies the opportunity for self-discovery, resilience, and ultimately, triumph. The "Rejection" book stands as a testament that, with the right mindset, rejection can become a springboard to reach new heights, unlock untapped potential, and transform dreams into reality.

www.ingramcontent.com/pod-product-compliance
Lightning Source LLC
Chambersburg PA
CBHW070905220526
45466CB00005B/2133